GANESHA

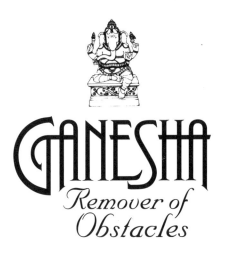

GANESHA

Remover of Obstacles

by Manuela Dunn Mascetti

CHRONICLE BOOKS

SAN FRANCISCO

Text by Manuela Dunn Mascetti
Design by Bullet Liongson
Manufactured in China
Typeset in Perpetua

ISBN 0-8118-2681-3

Distributed in Canada by
Raincoast Books
9050 Shaughnessy Street
Vancouver, B.C. V6P 6E5

10 9 8 7 6 5 4 3 2 1

Chronicle Books LLC
85 Second Street
San Francisco, CA 94105
www.chroniclebooks.com

Table of Contents

Introduction

Who is Ganesha, the endearing elephant-faced god of
Hinduism, the most popular and universally adored of the
330 million deities of the Hindu pantheon? Pictures and
statues of Ganesha are everywhere in India: in shops, on
family altars, beside roads, inside rickshaws, at inter-
sections, in shrines at the entrances of villages and temples,
inside books. He is praised at the beginning of ceremonies
of worship and at marriages; songs of devotion to him break
the silence of the Indian dawn. But Ganesha's popularity
is not exclusive to India; in September 1995, the elephant
god started sipping milk, his favorite drink, in temples and
shrines all over the world. It all began when a man in New
Delhi dreamt that Ganesha was thirsty and craved a little
milk. In the early morning the man rushed to the temple
and persuaded the priest to allow him to offer milk on a
spoon to a stone statue of the elephant god. Miraculously,
the milk disappeared, drunk by thirsty Ganesha. Like all
such things in India, news of this miracle spread like
wildfire, and within hours reports poured in from all
corners testifying that statues of Ganesha were drinking
milk everywhere. Soon Hindus in New York rushed to their
temple and there too the miracle happened. Manisha Lund,

a college student who went to the Hindu temple in Queens, described it as a virtual stampede. When she offered milk to the god, "it was drunk up like someone was drinking it from a straw." In a few days the miracle had spread as far as Canada, Mauritius, Kenya, Australia, Bangladesh, Malaysia, the United Kingdom, Denmark, Sri Lanka, Nepal, Hong Kong, Trinidad, Guyana, and Italy. What could this phenomenon be? Statues of Ganesha, whose trunk had no nostrils, sucked up hundreds of pints of milk within a few hours, and yet no milk was seen to flow out of them. A miracle for sure, a quirky reminder of the elephant god's love of tricks and playfulness. Since then, Ganesha images and statuettes have proliferated in the United States and Europe; in the current popularity of everything Indian, singers such as Madonna have appeared in Ganesha T-shirts. With his chubby male body, four arms, broken tusk, and snake belt, Ganesha is touching hearts everywhere.

Despite Ganesha's increasing popularity, remarkably little is known about him, except perhaps that he is the son of Shiva, lord supreme of Hinduism, and that Parvati is Ganesha's beautiful mother. But Ganesha is a powerful god in his home country. Worshiped since Vedic times, he has presided over the agricultural age of the Indian subcontinent and led devotees through the technological and information eras. Today, Ganesha is as strong and as potent as ever. I have seen him guarding the doors of the offices of *Elle* magazine in Bombay as well as on the dashboard of the Maruti sports utility vehicles of middle-class New Delhians.

Ganesha reigns over our beginnings and our changes, always there when needed. This box you hold in your hands is a reminder of your own highest wisdom and of your innate power to change *karma*. Place Ganesha on the night-stand by your bed, on your home altar, on your desk at work, or wherever it looks beautiful. Every time you look at it, allow it to remind you of the unfolding of your spiritual power, of the power of change in your life, and of new beginnings waiting to happen. Ideally, Ganesha should sit peacefully in an empty space, so his presence can create a field of energy, a space for you to change, an atmosphere of serenity and of trust that will help show you that the highest aspirations are indeed attainable. Ganesha enfolds all things and all beings completely, and his presence in your life will introduce a new dimension of being and of living.

May the power of Ganesha be with you and guide you through life decisions, karmic tangles, dharma puzzles, broken hearts, and obstacles to bliss and fulfillment.

The Mythology of Ganesha
THE BIRTH OF GANESHA

Shall I be gone long? Forever and a day.
Where will I go? Ask my song.
—C. D. LEWIS

Shiva, one of the greatest of all Hindu gods, forms a triumvirate with Brahma and Vishnu, the *trimurti*, a single body divided in three godly shapes. Shiva is the god of destruction, the lord of ashes and oil, and the ultimate ascetic and protector of yogis. He is worshiped as the guru of all gurus, the destroyer of worldliness, the one who grants wisdom, and the embodiment of renunciation and compassion. His constant companion is Nandin, the white bull of *dharma*, the ultimate law, and at his command are the *ganas*, semidivine/semidemonic beings who follow him from place to place and carry out his orders. This motley crew of strange-faced creatures runs around in the wild woods, fickle-tempered like the banshees from Irish lore, alternately horrible or suspiciously pleasing.

Parvati, the Daughter of the Mountain, first heard of Shiva from her playmates when she was still a girl. Her father, Himavat, was made of rock and was as old as the mountain itself; her mother, Mena, had lived her life between palaces and gardens; and Ganga, her sister, was the holy river Ganges. Parvati chanced upon the great god when he was meditating in the jungle. Shiva lifted his eyes to her and recognized her beauty as a woman, but did not leave his deep state of meditation. Parvati, however, became ensorcelled at that first meeting and began educating herself in *tapas*, the heat and ardor of cosmic energy that humans can draw on to destroy all illusion. Her ascetic meditations caused a whirl of energy to traverse the jungle where Shiva lived, and he became interested in this girl who was teaching herself how to become divine. Until now, the death of his previous consort, Sati, had oppressed his memory and left him wandering aimlessly for eons in grief over her loss. So the god decided to marry the beautiful young Parvati. He stole her away from her father's house and took her to his abode on Mount Kailash, the holiest place in India. The two lived happily in the heavenly home; Shiva recited the Vedas to Parvati, and when he made love to her she became Shakti, the primordial energy. In Hindu mythology, Shiva and Parvati are often said to sit on clouds discussing the wisdom of the ancient *rishis*, the Hindu sages who live in caves in the Himalayas, and the laws of nature, illusion, and power.

But for Shiva, the eternal ascetic, Parvati was never enough. He would leave her alone from time to time and, naked but for a coating of dark sacrificial ash covering his body, would go off for long periods of meditation. Parvati never knew when he would be back and longed for a child to keep her company in these moments of loneliness. As the mother of the cosmos, the goddess wanted to experience creation. But Shiva told her that he would not father any being, for there was no death in him. As an ascetic, he could not entangle himself in the karmic relationship with a son born from his seed. Parvati, however, was determined to have a child, whether Shiva would be its father or not.

Once when Shiva had left his wife Parvati for a long time in order to meditate on Mount Kailash, she became lonely and longed to have a son who would give her love and protection. She rubbed the unguents on the surface of her limbs and out of this material she rubbed forth a being in the shape of a young man. She breathed him to life and placed him at the doorway of her bath, instructing him to admit no one.

Meanwhile, Shiva returned from his long meditations and arrived at Parvati's private chamber, but the young man blocked the way and refused to let him in. Not knowing that this guard was Parvati's creation, Shiva became angry and, after a battle,

*cut off the guard's head. Overhearing the commotion outside,
Parvati came out. When she saw what had happened, she was
overcome with grief and anger at what Shiva had done. She told
him that unless he restored her son with a new head she would
bring the universe to destruction. So Shiva sent his servants in
search of a new head. As they traveled north, the auspicious
direction, they found an elephant and cut off its head and
returned to place it on the vacant shoulders of Parvati's guardian
son. As the son revived, Shiva praised him and gave him the
name of Ganesha, and adopted him as his own son.*

    *Shiva then told all the gods and goddesses who had assem-
bled there that Ganesha must be worshiped before all undertakings
or these will come to ruin. Ganesha then became the Lord of
Obstacles and placed barriers against all who neglected to worship
him; he became the Lord of Beginnings and brought success
to all who remembered him. From that time on, Ganesha has
placed and removed obstacles from the paths of gods, demons,
and humans.*[1]

Ganesha was not born from the sexual union of Shiva
and Parvati—his birth was "without husband," *vina nayakena*.
From the day Ganesha was born, Parvati no longer feared
being alone. Whenever Shiva went off for one of his meditation retreats, Parvati would curl up in bed and dictate one
long story after another. Ganesha, who sat at her feet and

wrote them down, is believed to be the scribe of the *Mahabharata*, the longest Indian epic.

Shiva loved Ganesha deeply, and was divinely pleased when Ganesha chose to adorn himself with red clothing or earth—a reminder of the saffron or orange robes of monastic communities, and of the redness of the earth from which all things come and to which all things return—lingering symbols of his father's asceticism. Shiva, the immortal, by becoming the father of Ganesha, forms a link with mortality that goes no further than his son because Ganesha will have no progeny of his own.

Ganesha's creation from the bodily fluids of Parvati reaches deep into the Hindu imagery of creation, of Vedic rites in which Brahmin priests rub firesticks together to give birth to the holy flame, and of the churning of oceans of milk in Puranic cosmologies. In the Brahmanic tradition of ancestor worship, small figurines are made from earth, dirt, and clay in the shape of a body. On the first day the head is made, followed on successive days by the neck and shoulders, torso, limbs, genitals, and finally the digestive powers and thirst, enabling the ancestors to receive the food offerings from their living descendants. This echoes the making Ganesha, first the birth as a human baby, and then his becoming part animal/part god, linking the realms of the gods, animals, and humans. The myth of Ganesha's birth is woven into everyday ritual practice and is part of the fabric that links humankind and the Hindu gods into one grand design.

THE PROTECTOR OF PARVATI

He was often to be seen lying awake beside Parvati's bed. He was her mild and thoughtful guardian, trunk curled up on his round belly and one tusk broken. To his right he kept a stylus and an inkpot. Parvati couldn't help stroking him whenever she passed by. "You are my son. You're mine. I can't say that of anybody else."
—ROBERTO CALASSO, *Ka*

The elephant is an ambivalence of the wild and the tame. The Vedic poets were impressed by the animal's massive strength; huge and gray, the elephant resembles the dark clouds of refreshing and violent rain that feed and replenish the parched land yearly at monsoon time. The tame elephant, the paradigm of power domesticated, clears wild jungles to make room for human habitation, carries kings into battles and ceremonial procession, and in his tameness is a symbol of order. Another side of Ganesha's tame

character is his role as protector and guardian of Parvati's bedroom, a symbol of the holy shrine. In the Puranic cosmologies, elephants are said to be the guardians of the four directions and to hold the world of the gods on their backs and shoulders. They stand guard over the points of entry and prevent any evil or polluting forces from entering the world of the gods. This can be seen in many Hindu temples, where rows of elephants adorn friezes along the lowest levels of the structures and elephant statues or the animals themselves stand as guardians of temple thresholds.

In the city of Benares, the holiest city in India, the capacity of Ganesha as the guardian of the threshold is in full evidence. The city is laid out as a model of the cosmos in seven concentric circles. Each circle has a shrine to Ganesha at the four directions and at the four intermediate points, for a total of fifty-six Ganeshas schematically spreading out in the eight directional compass points. In the center of Benares is a great Ganesha temple. A pilgrim must pass through one chain after another of these threshold guardians in order to gain access to the holy temple.

The myth of Ganesha also mirrors the intimate relationship between mother and son, and evokes the delight with which Indian women indulge their young children. Hindu children, during their first year of life, are seldom separated from their mothers. Hindu children are revered and so develop a deep assurance of character from this early support. The relationship between mother and son is especially tender, creating in many sons a lifelong bond of affection and loyalty. Women saints and gurus in India are often called Ma—mother—by their disciples.

SEXUALITY AND GANESHA

Shiva, Parvati, and Ganesha form a powerful triangle of passions. Before jealous Shiva cuts off his head, Ganesha is a beautiful young man, standing guard at his mother's threshold. Her private chambers—the bath and bedroom—symbolize her shrine, womb, and point of sexual entry, the place of simultaneous union and separation. When Shiva the husband is trying to get in, Ganesha prevents him and a great battle of passion and jealousy ensues. The father prevails, cutting off the young man's head in a great mythological symbol of castration, but restores him with the gift of a noble animal's head. Ganesha in his new guise is sexually ambiguous; his great long trunk reminds us of a powerful phallus, but his chubby body echoes a boy's eternal attachment to his mother. Shiva's symbol is the lingam, the creative phallus found in so many Indian temples, and Ganesha's

trunk is a reminder of his father's great creative powers. Ganesha submits to his father's rightful role as lover of Parvati and accepts his own role as Remover of Obstacles from the intimate chambers of Parvati. He becomes a yogi (an ascetic who abstains from sexual activities) and a dancer like his father in his incarnation as Shiva Nataraj, lord of the eternal dance of creation. He also takes up various weapons to guard his parents' doorway, protecting their intimacy from intruders. Ganesha's sacrifice both destroys him and makes him; when he is restored and given primacy of place before all other gods, Shiva and Parvati are reunited, death in the family is kept away, and there comes a new beginning. Subsequently, in the myth, Parvati uses her son as a sexual shield. When Shiva returns from his long ascetic absences full of lust and desire, she places Ganesha at the door of her private chambers to face his father alone. Ganesha becomes a sort of plaything in this divine marriage. Parvati's alienation from Shiva deepens her bond with her son and encourages him to remain the eternal boy. In Maharashtra, the Indian state where Ganesha is most worshiped, it is said that Ganesha never marries because he is unable to find another woman as beautiful as his mother, and so he remains at the crossroads (where his shrines are always located) waiting for one to come along.

Ganesha's equivocal sexual role can be traced to the powerful nature of elephants and their position in Indian royal and sacred life. On the one hand, the elephant is a symbol of sexuality incarnate. With few exceptions, all elephants in Hindu myths appear to be male. The phallus of the elephant is one of the biggest in the animal kingdom, and thus Ganesha symbolizes great fertility and eroticism. A rutting elephant is the embodiment of violent passion, thrashing and destroying everything in his path to get to his mate. The ichor, a thick, saplike secretion that oozes from the elephant's temples during the season of mating, is said to be so delicious that it intoxicates the bees buzzing around it so that they foolishly cast aside all risks in order to taste the elixir of erotic desire: "Forgetful of the lotuses and disregarding what the ear-stroke of the elephant will do, this honey-gatherer desires the pungent ichor. Fly on craving costs the addict bee her life." (D. H. H. INGALLS, *An Anthology of Sanskrit Court Poetry*)

On the other hand, the elephant is the protector of sacred temples and the prized animal of Maharajas. In his tame character, the elephant's strength is seen not as sexual but as protective of sacredness. In Hindu mythology, gods often represent what may appear to be contradictory qualities, not being entirely one thing or another. Ganesha

is most worshiped as the great protector, the one who
has forsaken his sexual power to become the guardian of
temples and of the gods. In sublimating his sexuality and
in not posing a sexual threat to his father, Ganesha has
found a role for himself among gods and goddesses.

HOW GANESHA BROKE HIS TUSK

Parasurama, "Rama with an ax," went into battle against
the Ksatriyas, the warrior caste that had been tyrannically
governing the world. Shiva had given him a magic ax to
defeat them and their demon army so he would be successful in returning the world to the rule of the Brahmins, the
priestly caste.

 After the successful battle, when Parasurama returned
to Shiva's palace to tell him of his success, he saw Ganesha
sitting in front of his parents' chamber, adorned with jewels
and sitting on cushions studded with gems. He bowed in
front of the elephant god, and just as he was about to enter
the most private palace chambers, Ganesha said to him,
"Wait, the Lord is there sleeping with Parvati. I will ask
their permission and then take you in there with me. Wait
a moment, brother."

 Being in a hurry, Parasurama said, "As soon as I have

gone inside and paid homage to these two parents of the universe, I will return immediately to my own palace. It was because of Shiva's power that I have been able to slay the many armies of demons, which were strong in their powers of delusion." But Ganesha replied, "You will have your audience, but today the Lord is in there with the goddess. You see, when a man and a woman are having intercourse, whoever disturbs their peace will surely go to hell—especially when it is one's parents, or guru, or king, or twice-born. Anyone who sees someone else's lovemaking will certainly lose his own life for seven births. And whoever sees the buttocks, breasts, or face of someone else's wife, mother, sister, or daughter is the worst kind of person."

Hearing this Parasurama became enraged and shouted, "Don't you think I know that? Have you lost your senses, are you trying to make some kind of joke, or did those words just slip out of your mouth? This injunction from the Shastras [priests] is meant for those who are unstable and filled with lust; but there is no sin for one who is without desire. So I will go into their bedroom and you, little boy, can stay here!" And with these words, he prepared to break into the divine chamber, but Ganesha immediately jumped up and blocked his way.

A great battle ensued between them, and Parasurama picked up his magical ax and got ready to throw it. But Ganesha lifted him up with his trunk and lowered him through the seven regions of the world into the ocean and the innermost part of the world. When they resurfaced, because they had been whirling so much, Ganesha thought his opponent had been defeated. But just then, Parasurama threw his ax at him and broke his left tusk in two. Hearing the great commotion, Shiva and Parvati came out of their chamber. When she heard what had happened, Parvati became enraged and blamed Shiva for all of it: "This Parasurama is more like a son to you than Ganesha. You gave him his ax to conquer the world and now he gives you the broken tusk of Ganesha as a further offering. So you take care of him because you are his great guru and he will do your household chores for you. I will stay here not a moment longer. I will take my son and go to my father's house." And so she left Shiva and Parasurama standing.[2]

It was Shiva's ax that broke Ganesha's tusk, just as it was Shiva's jealousy that beheaded Ganesha. Ganesha in this myth seems to regard the loss of his tusk as a matter of divine necessity, for something must be lost by the son who protects his parents in the tenderness of their copulation. This event is a reminder of the Indian Shastric rules that warn of the consequences of incest and voyeurism in one's own family, especially one's mother when she is engaged in sexual intercourse. In a country where families sleep together in one room for years, these rules are extremely necessary and remind Hindus of restraint and purity of intent.

Although the wound can be healed, Ganesha's tusk cannot be replaced and Shiva is then forced to make his son the leader of the *ganas*, his troop of demons. This myth echoes again the theme of anger and reconciliation between father and son, and Ganesha's eternal devotion to his mother by which he risks mutilation in order to protect her sexuality.

The mythology of Ganesha is rich in metaphoric meanings; we find tales of divine birth, beheading, sacrifice, threshold initiation, protection and guardianship, and elephant lore and worship. Ganesha's tales give us insight into the complex Hindu pantheon, infecting us with India's passion for color and paradox. With his investiture as both Remover of Obstacles and as Chief of the Demons, Ganesha leaves the shadow of his illustrious parents and attains his own unique identity.

GANESHA AND THE DEMONS

Ganesha is similar in form to the *yakshas*—semidivine, usually benevolent beings who attend Kubera, god of the spirits of darkness and of treasures and wealth. The *yakshas* live at the boundaries and bases of temples and help maintain an auspicious environment for deities and devotees alike. Kubera himself has a short, fat body like Ganesha's and a tusklike mustache. Many strands of Hindu myths link Ganesha to the demons, even though he was elevated to divine status by Shiva when he was invested with his role of protector of Parvati and acknowledged as Shiva's son. But to come from demonic stock is not necessarily disadvantageous in Hindu mythology. The demons are not all bad; they compete with the gods over the *soma* (the juice of the intoxicating plant) and the *amrita* (the elixir of eternal life) that are made by the churning of the oceans. They also perform mighty acts of asceticism to win boons from the gods, which enable them to destroy the universe and undermine the *dharma*, or law of existence. But the demons also sacrifice themselves and become transformed into beings of divine stature.

In order to rule over the *yakshas* and the *ganas*, Shiva's troops, one must understand their fickle nature. Ganesha can do so because he is himself part animal and part god.

One of his mythical names is Vinayaka, which means "to lead away," and refers to the groups of malevolent creatures who lead people astray and place obstacles in their paths. As their chief, Ganesha can help anyone ban these malefic influences which are endlessly plaguing mankind. These spirits can manifest as distractions on the spiritual path, as infidelities in marriage, as greed in business exchanges, and as ambition in social interactions. They can also negatively influence all matters of personal virtue and place obstacles in the way of auspicious marriages, healthy childbirth, political rule, scholarly attainment, and profitable business. These trickster spirits can only be appeased through appealing to Ganesha's benevolence. In India today, people call on the services of a Brahmin priest to free them from the *vinayakas*, and whole villages plagued by a bout of bad luck will enact rituals to clear the four corners of malefic influences.

Ganesha mediates between the opposing forces of the divine and the demonic. He understands the demons, knows their ways, and does not fear their powers. He stands both inside and outside the divine worlds, as he dwells at the threshold. He both places and removes obstacles and facilitates and thwarts undertakings. He does not tolerate neglect from demons, gods, or humans; those who fail or forget to pay him homage find their efforts coming to ruin.

LORD OF BEGINNINGS AND REMOVER OF OBSTACLES

Hear, O Parvati, what this son of yours will become. He will be like me in might, heroism, and compassion. This son of yours will become one just like me because of these qualities. He will make obstacles that last until death for those evil and impious ones who hate the Veda and the dharma. Those who fail to pay homage to me and Vishnu, the supreme lord, will go to great darkness by the obstacles laid before them by this lord of obstacles. In their houses there shall be quarrels without end. Because of the obstacles your son makes, everything perishes utterly. For those who do not worship, who are intent upon lies and anger, and are committed to fierce savagery, he will create obstacles. He will remove obstacles from those who revere the traditions, knowledge, and teachers. Without worshiping him, all actions and laws will become obstructed.

—SKANDA PURANA, 1.2.278-314[3]

Myriad Hindu myths tell the tales of Ganesha's powers to either place or remove obstacles from people's paths. His chief concern is to guard the well-being of the gods and their divine duties, thus being key to the proper function of the universe. Sometimes, however, as we learn in the following tale, Ganesha acts as a trickster spirit and places obstacles before the gods to teach them a lesson:

The gods were churning the oceans until, much to their surprise,
poison began to spill out. Narada, a rishi and the son of Brahma,
the first god of the Hindu trinity, warned them at the beginning
that they should pay homage to Shiva, but so eager were they to
obtain the soma that they ignored the warning. Soon the poison
spilled out, infecting the upper regions, and the gods, sages,
and demons fled in all directions, eventually taking refuge with
Brahma. But Brahma could do nothing to help them and directed
them instead to Vishnu, the second god of the Hindu trinity, but
he was also powerless to stop the burning poison from destroying
everything. Finally the gods came to Shiva and asked him for help.

Ganesha, who secretly had had a strong hand in creating
this huge problem, said to Shiva, "I have created this obstacle.
Because of fear and illusion the gods have not been worshiping
you or me, and I have put terrible obstructions in their actions."

Shiva then said to the gods, "Even though this world is
thought to be perishable, there is also that which is imperishable.
What is the use of sacrifice, asceticism, or undertaking any
action? Together you attempted the difficult task of churning
the oceans to obtain the soma. But you excluded and ignored
me in the process, and that's why your enterprise has gone
awry. Ganesha was created to bring every action to a successful
conclusion, but you did not honor him, and that's why you are
now so afflicted with difficulties." [4]

In this tale, mischievous Ganesha turns the *soma* that is created by the gods' churning of the oceans into poison to teach them a lesson because they have failed to worship him and his father. The *soma* is the intoxicating juice that gives the gods their supernatural powers and is the elixir of eternal life. By turning it into poison, the gods become ill with the very substance that they love so much and their world burns with the terrible venom the elephant god has created. By failing to honor Ganesha, the gods do not propitiate a good outcome to their making of the *soma*. Even the universe cannot function unless Ganesha is properly worshiped and asked to remove obstacles. This episode leads all the distressed gods to Shiva, who uses this occasion to remind them how the universe works and of the proper ways of worshiping Ganesha.

In looking at these myths of obstacles, we see Ganesha's fluidity of action: he places obstacles in front of gods, demons, and humans, but he also removes them. Ganesha's place in the divine scheme of things as well as in our personal *karma* is to do the same. This is his particular territory and the reason for his creation. From the beginning, Ganesha's energies are to be spent defending the spiritual and cosmological status quo: protecting the gods, routing demons, attending to our needs, and making sure that the flow of sacred power moves fluidly between the material plane and the domain of the gods. Ganesha, the gatekeeper, removes obstacles from the gods and places them instead before humans. Or he deludes our minds with desire, and poses challenges to our spiritual quest. He is testing our mettle. He doesn't corrupt the shrine itself, but challenges those who come to it with corrupt spirits.

We can make use of Ganesha's strategy of delusion by calling on his help in our own lives, building an altar to him, and getting him on our side. If we are suffering from the obstacles of separation from a beloved or contemplating a business opportunity, we should seek refuge in Ganesha's benevolence. Through him we can revoke *karma*, manifest desire, outwit opponents, gain the advantage, and banish trickster spirits. For the devotee, the act of worshiping or remembering Ganesha is both a gesture of gratitude for his protection and of propitiation for his noninterference in the successful completion of the undertaking. Ganesha gains us entry into the inner sanctum, the chamber of our desire, and lends power to the interminable process of action and consequence. In ruling the concrete world of actions and their fruits, success and failure, triumph and pain, Ganesha has become one of the most popular and beloved gods in the world. He is firmly here in our own reality and available at your door.

Ganesha's Powers

May we know the single-tusked one,
may we meditate on the one with the curved trunk.
May that tusked one inspire that
knowledge and meditation of ours.

—GANESHA GAYATRI [5]

The rites and forms of devotion associated with propitiating
Ganesha's powers are reflected in the tradition of Brahmanic
practices that grew out of the myths of the elephant god.
Ganesha's power is to place and remove obstacles at the
boundaries of time and space—temporarily at the beginning, and spatially at the threshold. These are the points of
entry, the places of highest possibility, where human desire
meets the unknown and interjects the destiny that is mapped
out for us by the gods. We bring to our undertaking motiva-
tion, awareness, and desire—*karma*. Therefore, any action
is unpredictable and vulnerable in its outcome, and with
Ganesha we may be able to grant it success. By appealing to
him at the beginning and at the threshold, we approach his
powers as if we were at a shrine; we think about what we
are about to do and demand that it be blessed. And because

Ganesha is part god, part animal, part demon, part child, and part human, he can mediate in all realms, connecting multiple worlds.

THE FIVE POWERS

When Hindus talk about the power emanating from a god or an incarnation of a holy spirit, they refer to the real phenomenon of *shakti*—a positive stream of energy whose vibrations can be felt both physically and spiritually. *Shakti* is partly what draws so many Westerners to Indian holy men and women, who transmit this power to devotees by touching the third eye, by an embrace, or simply by their physical presence. *Shakti* can feel like a small but powerful electrical current that jolts you into a feeling of well-being and peacefulness and awakens you to a dimension of profound understanding. *Shakti* is like a thunderbolt of light that makes your cells vibrate at a higher, more refined rate. All Hindu divinities transmit *shakti* to their devotees.

Ganesha's *shakti* has to do with the same elements found in his myth: the household regarded as shrine; the protection of the family, particularly of women; the extended protection of those who form the family; and the abundance that devotion brings. Five main streams of positive vibratory energies emanate from Ganesha at all times:

- The power to make your home a sanctuary and a haven of well-being
- The power to protect everyone in your immediate family and your friends, removing the obstacles that cause disharmony
- The power to bring harmony and abundance to all your relationships in the realms of work and business exchanges, and the power to influence income and charitable donations
- The power to be creative, enhancing the love of culture and devotion to religious practice
- The power to combine the first and third powers, and to bring great abundance to your life, both materially and spiritually, and to protect this abundance from trickster influences

THE THIRTY-TWO FORMS OF GANESHA

Hindu gods have lived and played from the beginning and through all the different cycles of cosmic time, which are called *yugas* in Sanskrit. According to the sacred scriptures, there have been four *yugas*, or ages of the world. Each *yuga* must be multiplied by 360 to obtain the sum in human years. Each age is preceded by a dawn (*sandhya*) and followed by a

dusk (*sandhyansha*) of equal length. We are currently in the fourth age, Kali Yuga, which is already 432,000 years old. Hindu gods live through each age, taking different forms at different times, either according to need or just for fun. Each aspect of a Hindu deity is given a different name because it symbolizes a specific characteristic. In Hinduism, to give someone a name is one of the most important sacred rites and resembles a rite of passage; it signifies the outer expression of an inner refinement and grace and is the first step leading to spiritual perfection.

Ganesha traditionally has thirty-two forms, which are listed and illustrated below under his Sanskrit name, Ganapati.

	1. *Bāla Gaṇapati*—This is the childlike manifestation of the god. In his hands he holds a banana, mango, sugarcane, and jackfruit, all representing the earth's abundance.
	2. *Taruṇa Gaṇapati*—This is the red eight-armed god, symbolizing youth and holding a noose and goad, *modaka* (his favorite sweet), a wood apple, a rose apple, his broken tusk, a sprig of paddy, and a sugarcane stalk.

3. *Bhakti Gaṇapati*—Shining like the full moon during harvest season and garlanded with flowers, this is the manifestation dear to devotees. He holds a banana, mango, coconut, and a bowl of *payasa* pudding.

4. *Vīra Gaṇapati*—Ganesha as the valiant warrior assumes a fierce, commanding pose, with sixteen arms and a variety of weapons: a goad, discus, bow, arrow, sword, shield, spear, mace, battle-ax, trident, and more.

5. *Śakti Gaṇapati*—Four-armed and seated with one of his *shaktis* (a female magical attendant) on his knees, this Ganesha guards the household.

6. *Dvija Gaṇapati*—Four-headed and the color of the moon, this Ganesha reminds us of the urgency of disciplined striving.

7. *Siddhi Gaṇapati*—Golden-yellow, Siddhi Ganesha epitomizes achievement and self-mastery.

8. *Ucchishṭa Gaṇapati*—This is the lord of sacred offerings and the guardian of culture.

9. *Vighna Gaṇapati*—This lord of obstacles is of brilliant gold, bedecked in jewels.

10. *Kshipra Gaṇapati*—The "quick-acting" Ganesha, giver of boons, holds the *kalpavriksha* (wish-fulfilling) tree in his hand.

11. *Heramba Gaṇapati*—Five-faced and white-bodied, this protector of the weak rides on a lion.

12. *Lakshmī Gaṇapati*—This giver of success sits flanked by Wisdom and Achievement.

13. *Mahā Gaṇapati*—This is the Great Ganesha, who is accompanied by his *shaktis*.

14. *Vijaya Gaṇapati*—This is the four-armed, red-hued, victorious bestower of success.

15. *Nṛitya Gaṇapati*—The "happy dancer."

16. *Ūrdhva Gaṇapati*—This is the "elevated" elephant god.

17. *Ekākshara Gaṇapati*—With his hand extended in offering, this is the giving manifestation of Ganesha.

18. *Varada Gaṇapati*—Ganesha as the boon-giving deity whose third eye projects wisdom.

19. *Tryakshara Gaṇapati*—The lord of "three letters" (A-U-M).

20. *Kshipra Prasāda Gaṇapati*—The "quick rewarder," who presides from a *kusha* grass throne. His big belly symbolizes the manifest universe.

21. *Haridrā Gaṇapati*—This is the elegant, posh Ganesha.

22. *Ekadanta Gaṇapati*—He has a single tusk and holds an ax in one of his hands to cut the bonds of ignorance.

23. *Sṛishṭi Gaṇapati*—This is the lord of "happy manifestations."

24. *Uddaṇḍa Gaṇapati*—This is "enforcer" of *dharma*, the laws of being.

25. *Ṛiṇamochana Gaṇapati*—The remover of humanity's bondage.

26. *Ḍhuṇḍhi Gaṇapati*—This much-sought Ganesha holds a small pot of precious gems thought to represent the treasury of awakening.

27. *Dvimukha Gaṇapati*—The "two-faced," who sees in all directions.

 28. *Trimukha Gaṇapati*—This three-faced god gestures protection with one right hand and blessings with a left.

 29. *Simha Gaṇapati*—Riding astride a lion, he symbolizes strength and fearlessness.

 30. *Yoga Gaṇapati*—The lord of meditation.

31. *Durga Gaṇapati*—The "savior," who waves the flag of victory over darkness.

32. *Saṅkaṭahara Gaṇapati*—The dispeller of sorrow.

SACRED SYMBOLS

Ganesha has many sacred symbols associated with him. Some represent his power as the favorite animal of *maharajas*, or his purity (elephants, despite their size, are pure vegetarians), his wisdom, his benevolence, or his ability to place and remove obstacles. These symbols are also sacred objects that you can collect during your travels in the Orient or simply gather on your altar to keep him happy and to perform a sacred function for you: a bowl of sweets, a mace, a Churi dagger, the mala prayer beads, a pot of nectar, an arrow, a sugarcane bow, a lotus flower, a *vina* (Indian lute), a goblet, a water vessel, and many more. These are sacred objects highly esteemed in India, almost like shamanic tools, as well as symbols that remind us of psychic patterns. For instance, the coconut is the symbol of the ego—soft and sweet inside, hard and rough outside. Breaking a coconut and placing it on your altar at the feet of Ganesha will help you break the ego's hold on someone or a situation.

ANKUSA *Gold*—Loving Ganesha's deliberate mind moves dullards ahead in their birth *karmas* whenever they tarry. He goads on all souls who are moving too slowly with his *ankusa*.

KAMANDALU *Water Vessel*—Loving Ganesha, dear to disciples, has their water vessel. Symbol of fullness, giving devotees all needs, *kamandalu* eternally pours, never needing to be filled.

MODAKAPATRA *Bowl of Sweets*—Loving Ganesha is said to have a sweet tooth, or tusk. But the *modaka* ball is a symbol of what he loves most: *moksha*, liberation, the sweetest of all sweet things.

ÇHURI *Dagger*—Loving Ganesha sometimes holds the dagger, keenly sharp, likened to the "razor's edge," the narrow and sometimes difficult path the spiritual aspirant must walk.

PUSHPASARA *Flower Arrow*—Loving Ganesha shoots flower-covered arrows from his sugarcane bow in guidance to devotees so they will not wander too far from *dharma's* path of true fulfillment.

CHĀMARA *Fly-Whisk Fan*—Loving Ganesha sits, as he always does, whisking away the past within the minds of devotees, young and old, rich and poor, educated and practical.

PARAŚU *Ax*—Loving Ganesha knows there are difficult times ahead for some of his devotees. He protects them from evils they have attracted with his *parasu*.

ŚAṄKHA *Conch*—Loving Ganesha listens to the *puja's* conch sound loudly, reminding him of elephants calling happily in the jungle. He declares, "Come hither to be with me and pray."

THE SOUNDLESS SOUND—AUM

That word is Aum.
This syllable is the imperishable spirit,
This indeed is the highest end.
Knowing this syllable, truly indeed,
Whatsoever one desires will be his...
That is the Supreme Support,
Knowing that support,
One becomes happy in the Brahma world.

—KATHA UPANISHAD 2.15-16

When we draw the sacred symbol for *aum*—the soundless
sound of the universe that hums and makes everything
vibrate in harmony—we see that it resembles two elephants
in embrace. There is a beautiful story associated with
Ganesha and *aum*: When Shiva and Parvati were in the
celestial audience hall, the paintings they saw on the walls
represented the two sacred syllables *a* and *u*, which together
resembled two elephants making love forming the syllable
aum. This syllable has special associations with Ganesha
and also resembles the face of a single elephant; with the
a depicting the head and belly, the *u* depicting the trunk,
and the *anusvara* (the *m*) the plate of sweet fruits offered
to him. *Aum* is also a symbol of the origin of movement

from abstract sound and calligraphic form to embodied
existence that is associated with Ganesha's divinity.

ॐ विनायकाय नमः	Aum Vināyakāya Namaḥ *Adoration to the remover of obstacles*
ॐ अग्निगर्वच्छिद्दे नमः	Aum Agnigarvacchide Namaḥ *Adoration to Him who destroyed the ego of the fire*
ॐ इन्द्रश्रीप्रदाय नमः	Aum Indraśrīpradāya Namaḥ *Adoration to the restorer of India's wealth*
ॐ वाणीप्रदाय नमः	Aum Vāṇīpradāya Namaḥ *Adoration to Him who gives the power of speech*
ॐ सर्वतनयाय नमः	Aum Sarvatanayāya Namaḥ *Adoration to the bestower of all fulfillment*
ॐ सर्वात्मकाय नमः	Aum Sarvātmakāya Namaḥ *Adoration to Him who is the soul of all*
ॐ बुद्धिप्रियाय नमः	Aum Buddhipriyāya Namaḥ *Adoration to Him who is fond of intelligence*
ॐ शान्ताय नमः	Aum Śāntāya Namaḥ *Adoration to the peaceful one*

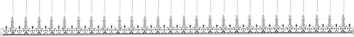

Ganesha Puja

Just as rivers flowing to the ocean merge in it,
Losing their name and form,
So the wise individual, freed from name and form,
manifests the Divine.
Do you identify with the drop of water or
with the water of the drop?

—JOHN GRIMES

Hindus worship Ganesha in all manners, through public
and private prayers and meditations, singing devotional
songs, calendrical rites and vows (governed by the moon),
as well as the building and visiting of sacred shrines. The
main spiritual home of Ganesha in India is Maharashtra,
the cultural and political state surrounding Bombay (now
renamed Mumbai), which occupies about one hundred
thousand square miles. Although many temples are dedi-
cated to him all over India, in Maharashtra Ganesha is not
just guardian of the threshold, but the main deity in many
shrines.

There are two forms of worship for Hindus: private
and public. The word *puja* simply translated means
"worship," and it can take on an infinite variety of forms.

Most families in Maharashtra will have a small altar with a clay statuette of the elephant god whose spirit dwells in the household. The family members light incense sticks every morning at dawn and every evening at dusk and make food offerings of Ganesha's favorite sweets, which can be eaten later as *prasad*, or divine food that has been imbued with his divine qualities. Children may clothe Ganesha statues, give the god gifts, entertain him with songs, and treat him as if he were the most valuable and royal of guests. In India, Ganesha is worshiped at a very intimate level of family life. He oversees and helps with the problems people contend with every day, not just great spiritual ambitions, and so is regarded more as a friend than as an all-powerful god high in his heavens.

Public worship of Ganesha is called *utsava*, or festival, and takes the forms of processions and religious and entertainment programs inside Ganesha temples throughout India, particularly in Maharashtra. Family and temple statues of Ganesha are carried in procession to the river, where they are cleansed. With the Hindus' religious effervescence, these occasions turn into an opportunity for great festivities. The festivals honor religious tradition, celebrate change, and bring private worship out into the streets in recognition of Ganesha's power to embrace everyone. The same themes of the familial and the intimate are carried through from the home to the *utsava*, with families joining the procession to the river for a great merry-all of elephant-god worship.

BUILDING YOUR GANESHA SHRINE

Creating a home shrine is not difficult. The altar should be close to the floor, since most *pujas* are performed seated. It's good to cover your altar with a beautiful textile—maybe a cloth you have brought back from India, or some sort of covering that will establish the sacred ground. Place the statuette in the center of the altar. *Puja* implements are kept on a tray, which should also be special and reserved only for this occasion. In India, people use metal trays, where they keep *ghee* (clarified butter), lamps, bells, cups, spoons, and small pots that are easily available from Indian household shops and are never used for anything other than *pujas*. Some necessary items include the following: two cups for holding water, a small vase or basket of fresh flowers, an oil lamp or candle that will remain lit during the whole *puja*, a lamp with a cotton wick for waving the flame around the deity, a small bell, an incense burner and a few incense sticks, a small container with sandalwood paste,

and some fresh fruit or a bowl of cooked rice. You may want to dress your Ganesha or adorn him with garlands. The room will ideally have a CD player so you can listen to meditation music while performing the *puja*, and some additional candles to cast a relaxing atmosphere while you are in prayer.

INSTRUCTIONS FOR HOME AND OFFICE PUJAS

As the Remover of Obstacles, Ganesha should be an important presence in your office and in your thoughts about beginning a new professional enterprise. In India, most offices have an image of Ganesha—on top of doorways in shops and offices, in a special niche, or in framed photographs or lithographs. In Maharashtra, Ganesha graces even the stalls of *chai-wallahs*, the tea vendors at street corners, and schoolchildren often write a Ganesha mantra at the top of their examination papers to get good results.

While you prepare your *puja*—lacing the flowers on the altar, lighting candles, and preparing food offerings—it is important that you quiet your mind, maybe by listening to meditation music or reciting a mantra. This preparation is necessary for the good results of your *puja*. Approach Ganesha devotionally, as though you were about to meet someone very special and holy. Purify your mind from all thoughts of problems, work, anger, and troubles, and begin to turn it to meditation and silence. *Puja* is a yoga, or union, with the divine.

When you have everything ready, sit cross-legged in front of or to the left of the altar (on the deity's right). Close your eyes, breathe deeply, and sit quietly, attuning your nervous system to meditation and to the sacred act you are about to perform. All offerings in your ritual should be made with the right hand; when this is done correctly it becomes a beautiful gesture of grace.

You can make up your own prayers and mantras for Ganesha and personalize your ritual, finding your own way to create a dialogue and be intimate with the beautiful elephant god. In the following section you will find a selection of traditional Hindu mantras and prayers if you prefer to begin and end with ancient sacred words.

MANTRAS, PRAYERS, AND SONGS

Pujas create or invoke their own worlds of meaning. At the center of each prayer, mantra, or devotional song there is an exchange between the human world of *samsara* and the spiritual world of *nirvana*. The latter is represented by

some object or symbol. The worshiper adopts the posture of surrender and through the performance of *puja* the two worlds of *samsara* and *nirvana* move closer together and may merge. As Ganesha—the symbol of the "other reality"— receives devotion and offerings of mantras and prayers, the worshiper gains spiritual and material enhancement. There are benefits from their mutual interaction. *Puja* is the expression of the very ancient Brahmanic sacrificial tradition that elaborates the creation of every form and manifestation out of the sacrificed form of the divine. Ganesha always reciprocates mantras, prayers, and gifts by bestowing the worshiper with his obstacle-removing powers. For an explanation of Sanskrit and Hindi pronunciation, see page 87.

Aum Vināyakāya Namaḥ
    Mantra for removing obstacles

Aum Avyayāya Namaḥ
    Mantra to appeal to the inexhaustible powers
    of Ganesha, to obtain endurance during a
    difficult enterprise

Aum Pūtāya Namaḥ
> Mantra in praise of the purity of Ganesha
> to make confusing issues become clear

Aum Dakshāya Namaḥ
> Mantra in praise of the skills of Ganesha

Aum Agnigarvacçhide Namaḥ
> Mantra for destroying the fire of ego

Aum Indraśrīpradāya Namaḥ
> Mantra for restoring divine wealth

Aum Vāṇīpradāya Namaḥ
> Mantra for rightful speech

Aum Sarvatanayāya Namaḥ
> Mantra for the bestowing of all fulfillment

Aum Sarvātmakāya Namaḥ
> Mantra for deepening soulful qualities

Aum Buddhipriyaya Namaḥ
> Mantra for the calling of intelligence

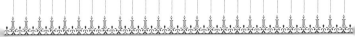

Aum Śāntāya Namaḥ
    Mantra for bringing peace

Aum Bhaktavighna-vināśanāya Namaḥ
    Mantra for the destruction of obstacles
    on friends' paths

Aum Śaktisaṁyutāya Namaḥ
    Mantra for increasing power

Aum Haraye Namaḥ
    Mantra for destroying evil with lionlike courage

Aum Kālāya Namaḥ
    Mantra for controlling destiny

Aum Kāmine Namaḥ
    Mantra for love

Aum Vītabhayāya Namaḥ
    Mantra for banishing fear

Aum Śrīdāya Namaḥ
    Mantra for bringing great wealth

Aum Śrīpataye Namaḥ
    Mantra for bringing overflowing wealth

Aum Kāntāya Namaḥ
    Mantra to appeal to the loved one

Aum Dayāyutāya Namaḥ
    Mantra for compassion

PRAYERS

AN ELEPHANT PRAYER

Everyone's heard of an elephant walk
And a few have listened to an elephant talk,
But this is a poem more special, more rare,
Than an African do made of elephant hair.

Two hands on the head beat an elephant prayer,
It's a gesture of hope when we tap ourselves there.
While onlookers see but a strange little knock,
Devotees swear it breaks any deadlock.

So, if you should worry or anguish or balk
When life gets you down or you meet a big block,
Whisper an Aum, and if you but dare,
Call on loving Ganesha who always is there.

Kassiyappa Sivacharya Kandapuranam

In order that your birth becomes free of its fetter, and you
Attain with ease human perfection on earth, worship, O man,
With devotion true the flowerlike feet of the triple-eyed,
*   elephant-faced divine guru,*
Ganapati, who grants without fail all your wishes.

Family Prayer

Oh divine beings of all three worlds,
Let us bring our minds to rest in
The darshana of Him who has one tusk.

Let us meditate upon Him who has the
Form of an elephant with a curved trunk.
May He guide us always along the right path.
Aum, peace, peace, peace, Aum.

Ganesha Gita

Gita means song. It can be sung alone or with others after
the recitation of mantras. Sing while you offer food to
bountiful Ganesha and he will become happy and joyful.

*O Ganesha, You are the red-colored leader
Of the ganas, the ocean of compassion,
O elephant-faced Lord.*

*The siddhas and charanas ever in your service,
The grantor of all attainment. O Vinayaka, we
Bow to you again and again.*

*Master of all arts of knowledge, the best one of all,
We bow to you again and again.*

*Big-bellied Lord who blesses all with prosperity,
Parvati's son, you are praised by all the gods.*

SWEET OFFERINGS

Offerings to deities are called *prasad* in Sanskrit and are a fundamental part of any devotional act or ritual. After *prasad* has been offered to Ganesha, the elephant god "returns" it to the worshiper to be shared as *prasada*, or spiritual food. The divine food, shared with Ganesha, will bond you with him. The word *prasad* is derived from the Sanskrit prefix *pra*, meaning "down," and the root *sad*, meaning "sit." In its barest meaning, *prasad* is a settling down, a growing clear, and a becoming satisfied. This is what happens when we allow the spiritual realm to influence our own lives. Ganesha's favorite *prasad* are sweet fruits, betel nuts, coins, and *modakas* (sweet flour balls).

Keep the Ganesha you have found in this box happy with offerings. Change them daily and delight him with surprising gifts. Remember: he is part child, part elephant, part human, part demon. He likes mischief and will be ever faithful if you love him like he was loved by the beautiful goddess Parvati and given status by the all-powerful god Shiva. May he bring you infinite blessings!

NOTES TO THE TEXT

[1] This retelling of the Hindi myth of Ganesha is from:
Courtright, Paul B. *Ganeśa: Lord of Obstacles, Lord of Beginnings*. New York and Oxford: Oxford University Press, 1985, p. 5.

[2] The breaking of Ganesha's tusk is paraphrased from:
Courtright, Paul B. *Ganeśa: Lord of Obstacles, Lord of Beginnings*. New York and Oxford: Oxford University Press, 1985, pp. 74-76.

[3] Shastri, J. L., and G. P. Bhatt, eds. *Skanda Purana: Ancient Indian Tradition and Mythology*, vols. 1-4. Delhi: Motital Banarsidass, 1992, p. 5.

[4] The story of the soma being transformed into poison by Ganesha is paraphrased from: Courtright, Paul B. *Ganeśa: Lord of Obstacles, Lord of Beginnings*. New York and Oxford: Oxford University Press, 1985, pp. 138-139.

[5] The "Ganesha Gayatri" is quoted from: Grimes, John. *Ganapati: Song of the Self*. Albany, NY: State University of New York Press, 1995, p. 27.

PRONUNCIATION AND SPELLING NOTE

Sanskrit and Hindi vowels are pronounced as in Italian—
except for a short *a*, which is pronounced like the *u* in the
English word "but"—the long *a* is pronounced like the *a*
in "father"; *e* and *o* are always long; *r* in Sanskrit is a vowel
and should be pronounced like the *ri* in "ring."

Consonants are pronounced as in English, with the
following cases being noted: c as in "church" for words in
Sanskrit; the j is pronounced as in "joy"; the *ś* and *ṣ* are
similar to the sound *sh* as in "shine." Ganesha is spelled with
sh throughout the book to reflect the English pronunciation
of the elephant god's name, though in Hindi or Marathi
(the language of Maharashtra) it is often spelled Ganeśa.
The latter form appears in quoted materials and in the
Bibliography where the Sanskrit spelling was used in the
title of books. Ganapati is the Sanskrit translation of Ganesha
and this is the name often used in mantras and *pujas*.

The aspirated consonants should be pronounced
distinctly: *th* as in "hothouse"; *ph* as in "top hat"; *gh* as in
dog house"; and *bh* in "clubhouse."

A Sanskrit-English distionary will give interested
readers and specialists both the phonetic translation of the
words and their transliteration. Titles recommended are

The Concise Sanskrit-English Dictionary by Vasudeo Govind (compiler) and Davidovic Mladen, published by Hippocrene Books; and A Concise Dictionary of Indian Philosophy: Sanskrit Terms Defined in English by John A. Grimes, published by State University of New York Press.

FURTHER READING LIST

Coomaraswami, A. K. Ganesha. Boston: Bulletin of the Museum of Fine Arts, 1928.

Courtright, Paul B. Ganeśa: Lord of Obstacles, Lord of Beginnings. New York and Oxford: Oxford University Press, 1985.

Grimes, John A. Ganapati: Song of the Self. Albany, NY: State University of New York Press, 1995.

Subramuniyaswami, Satguru Sivaya. Loving Ganesha: Hinduism's Endearing Elephant-Faced God. Himalayan Academy, 1996.

The Encyclopedia of Eastern Philosophy and Religion. Boston: Shambhala Publications, 1989.

ACKNOWLEDGMENTS

BOX IMAGE: *Elephant and Rider Trampling on Tiger*, Oudh, India, c. 1770, © The British Library, London.
Battle Between Shiva and Krishna Pahari, Kangra style, 1858, © British Museum, London

BOOK COVER: *Painting of Animals*, © The British Library, London

END PAPERS: *General View of Reliefs*, Hoysala dynasty, mid-12th century, Hoysalesvara Temple, Halebid, Karnataka (Mysore), India, © Vanni/Art Resource, New York

PAGE 2: *Ganesha and Goddess Riding on Tigers*, Kashmir, c. 1800, © The British Library, London

PAGE 6: *Shiva, Parvati, and Children*, c. 1760, © Victoria & Albert Museum, London

PAGE 10: *Shiva's Family*, Pahari, Guler style, c. 1760, © British Museum, London

PAGE 15: *Shiva and Parvati*, Chola period, 12th-14th centuries, India, © Werner Forman Archive Private Collection, New York

PAGE 18: *Ganesha on His Rat Preceded and Followed by Two Members of the Ganas*, Tanjore, South India, c. 1800, © British Museum, London

PAGE 21: *Shiva and Family at the Burning Grounds*, watercolor, Indian, Kangra style, c. 1810, © Victoria & Albert Museum, London

PAGE 22, BACKGROUND: Textile, Kincob, India, c. 19th century, © Victoria & Albert Museum, London. MAIN IMAGE: *Lady Listening to Girl Playing the Veena*, © The British Library, London

PAGE 24: *Ganesha*, © Victoria & Albert Museum, London

PAGE 27: *Shiva, Parvati, Nandin, and Ganesh*, reverse glass painting, end of 19th century, © British Museum, London

PAGE 29: An Indian poster of Ganesha, Robert Harding Library, London

PAGE 32: *Pancamukhi Ganesha*, by Banambar Nayak, © The British Museum, London

PAGE 34: *Ganesha*, © The British Library, London

PAGE 37: Ganesha shrine at Chitar Fort in Rajasthan, India, © Ann & Bury Peerless, Birchington-on-Sea, Kent

PAGE 41: *Ganesha*, © The British Library, London

PAGE 42, BACKGROUND: Block-printed cotton, 18th century, India, © Victoria & Albert Museum, London. MAIN IMAGE: Painting of Ganesha with Parvati, © The British Library, London

PAGE 46, BACKGROUND: Detail from the hem of a wedding shirt, embroidered with beetle skins (green) and tinsel in a diamond pattern, India, 19th century, © Victoria & Albert Museum, London. MAIN IMAGE: Bronze statue of Ganesha Tamil Nadu, India, Cola style, 11th-12th centuries, © Victoria & Albert Museum, London

PAGE 56: Statue of Ganesha, Hoysala period, 12th-13th centuries, Mysore, India, © De Young Museum, San Francisco/Werner Forman Archive

PAGE 60, BACKGROUND: Textile, Kincob, India, c. 19th century, © Victoria & Albert Museum, London. MAIN IMAGE: Lalita Durga between her two sons, Ganesha and Karttikeya, Eastern India, 11th century, basalt statue, © British Museum, London

PAGE 63: Painting of Ganesha, Kalighat, India, c. 1860, © British Museum, London

PAGE 64, BACKGROUND: Block-printed cotton, 18th century, India, © Victoria & Albert Museum, London. MAIN IMAGE: *Elephant Falling in Love with the Moon's Reflection in the Stream*, India, Mughal period, c. 1600, © The British Library, London

PAGE 68, BACKGROUND: Textile, Kincob, India, c. 19th century, © Victoria & Albert Museum, London. MAIN IMAGE: House wall sculpture of Ganesha, Sri Lanka, © Ancient Art and Architecture Collection, Pinner, UK

PAGE 71, BACKGROUND: Block-printed cotton, 18th century, India, © Victoria & Albert Museum, London. MAIN IMAGE: Statue of Ganesha from the Lakshmi Naranyam Temple in New Dehli, India, © Ann & Bury Peerless, Birchington-on-Sea, Kent

PAGE 72: Folk statue of nine-headed Ganesha

PAGE 75: *A Lover on a Caparisoned Elephant Holds Hands with a Lady at a Window under a Star-lit Sky*, Murshidabad, India, c. 1770-75, © The British Library, London

PAGE 76, BACKGROUND: Detail of a woman's dress, embroidered silk, Baluchistan, Pakistan, c. early-19th century, © Victoria & Albert Museum, London. MAIN IMAGE: Gods churning the oceans of milk, Southern India, c. 1830, © British Museum

PAGE 79: BACKGROUND: Detail of a woman's shawl embroidered with silk and sequins, Indus Kohistan, Pakistan, mid-20th century, © Victoria & Albert Museum, London. MAIN IMAGE: A sandstone statue of Ganesha, south-eastern Uttar Pradesh, c. 1750, © British Museum, London

PAGE 83: *State Entry of Indian Prince into a Citadel*, © The British Library, London

PAGE 84: BACKGROUND: Textile, Kincob, India, c. 19th century, © Victoria & Albert Museum, London. MAIN IMAGE: *Hindu Woman Worshipping at Ganesha Temple*, watercolor (for the East India Company), by a Lucknow artist, c. 1815-1820, © The British Library, London